Tom and Bella put up a tent on the grass.

Tom puts all his jungle animals in the tent.

Bella brings her doll and her rabbit to the tent.

Bella's doll and rabbit hit the jungle animals.

'Silly animals,' says Bella.
She puts them on the grass.

Tom sees all his jungle animals on the grass.

'Bella put my animals back in the tent,' says Tom.

He looks in the tent.

Oh no! It is full of dolls!